SUPER C

COLORING AND ACTIVITY BOOK

Images by Daniela Frongia
Activities based on the children's book
"Super Cooper Wins the Stanley Cup" by Jack Gates
www.triumphtogether.net

This book belongs to:

____

"WHO'S READY FOR SOME HOCKEY?"

Have you ever had to go to the doctor or stay in a hospital? On the lines below, write about how it made you feel to be there. Were you nervous or scared? How did you try to stay brave?

be brave

DREAMS

Draw a picture of yourself accomplishing one of your biggest dreams:

SOMEDAY I WILL PLAY HOCKEY!

Make A Hockey Game

Get your parents to help you. Grab some popsicle sticks, glue, scissors, tape, and even some magic markers. Cut the ends from two popsicle sticks and glue them to the bottoms of two other popsicle sticks to create a hockey stick. Add small pieces of colorful tape to the top and if you want, color your hockey stick to match your team's color. Grab a button and play hockey on the kitchen table!

HE SHOOTS!

HE SCORES!

Below, draw a picture of yourself playing your favorite sport...

I WISH TO PLAY!

I WISH TO PLAY!

SPORTS

WORD SEARCH

TENNIS	GOLF	BASKETBALL
FOOTBALL	VOLLEYBALL	YOGA
KARATE	GYMNASTICS	BOWLING
BADMINTON	RUNNING	SWIMMING

T	E	N	N	I	S	A	R	S	O	E	G	B	F
G	N	E	B	O	W	L	I	N	G	U	B	A	O
Y	N	F	P	U	I	B	U	G	O	L	F	S	O
M	Y	L	R	U	N	N	I	N	G	S	J	K	T
N	O	E	I	I	P	O	C	Q	I	Y	I	E	B
A	L	K	S	H	M	E	M	Z	R	F	N	T	A
S	B	A	D	M	I	N	T	O	N	I	G	B	L
T	V	R	S	E	A	U	T	I	H	G	L	A	L
I	G	A	V	O	L	L	E	Y	B	A	L	L	C
C	H	T	J	I	K	Y	O	G	A	O	S	L	A
S	F	E	A	S	W	I	M	M	I	N	G	R	S

Sometimes
LIFE IS HARD

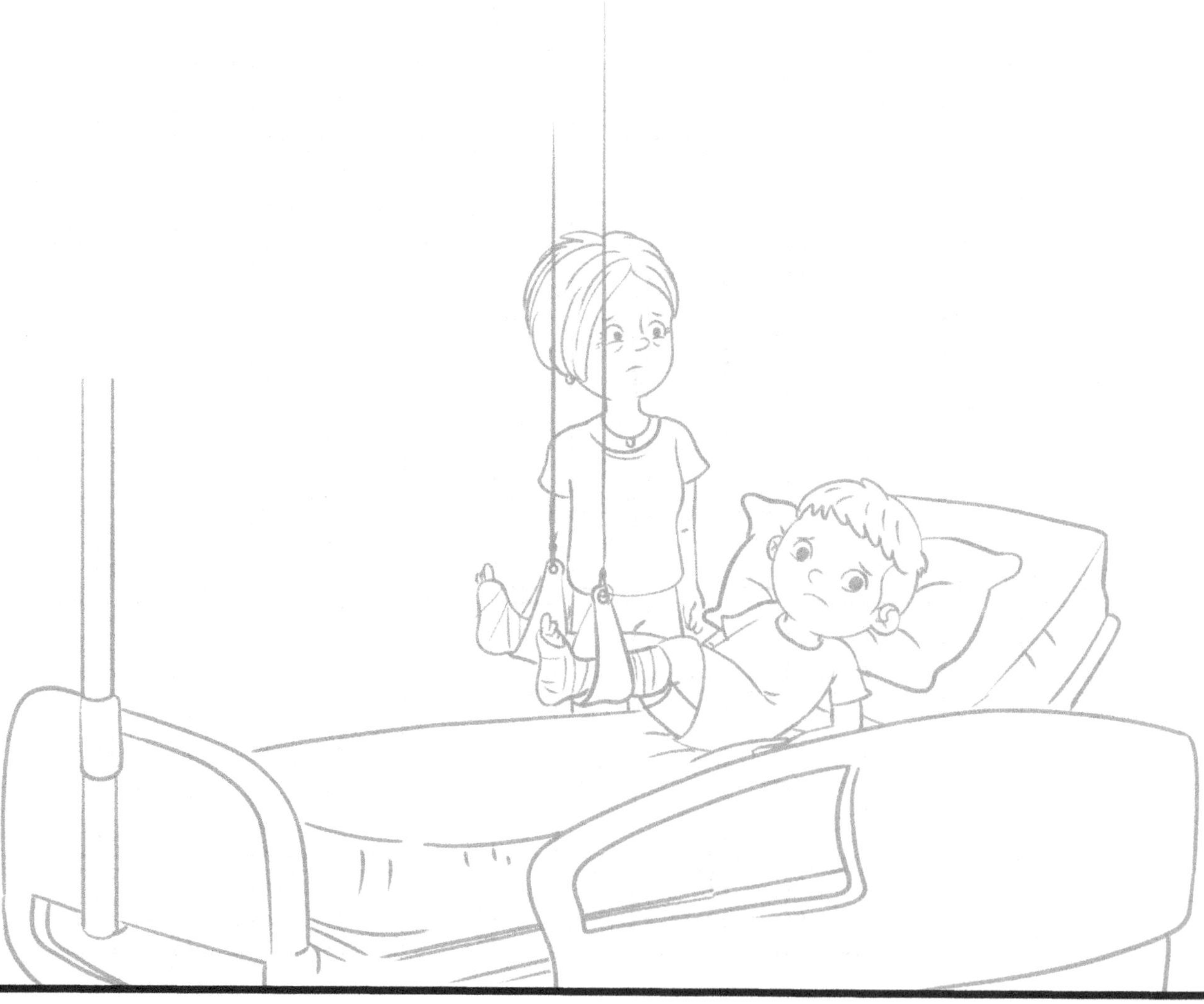

Sometimes
LIFE IS GOOD!

SPORTS TALKING POINTS

Play with your friends or your family. Sit in a circle and go one at a time choosing a card from below and then have a group chat about what the card says.

What's your favorite sport?

What's your least favorite sport?

What sports do you like to watch?

Who is your favorite athlete and why?

Who do you usually play sport with?

If you could play any sport as a pro, what would it be?

YOU CAN DO IT!

LET'S GO!

BE CREATIVE!

WHEREVER YOU ARE

Below, write about your friends:

Who is your best friend? ______________________________

What activities do you enjoy with your friends?

____

____

____

Where do you hang out with your friends?

____

____

____

How does having friends make your life better?

____

____

____

glue a photo of you with your best friend in the frame

FRIENDSHIP

best friends

EVERY SUPERHERO NEEDS A SIDEKICK

You're going to the

STANLEY CUP FINALS!

DREAMS DO COME TRUE!

HEROES

Let SUPER COOPER play!

Below write a story about a time when someone gave you a chance to do something BIG and it made you both excited and a little bit nervous...

Sometimes

WE FEEL SCARED

It's nice to have support

FROM A GOOD COACH

20
20

HE DID IT!

STANLEY CUP CHAMPIONS!

LET'S HEAR IT FOR SUPER COOPER

GOOD JOB, FRIEND!

REMEMBER...

BE BRAVE!

DREAM BIG!

BELIEVE IN YOURSELF!

Ashland Ink

Super Cooper's Coloring and Activity Book

Published by Ashland Ink Publishing
209 West 2nd Street #177
Fort Worth TX 76102
www.ashlandink.com

Published in the United States of America

ISBN: 978-1-963514-09-4

Made in the USA
Las Vegas, NV
21 September 2025

28338763R00024